D1006257

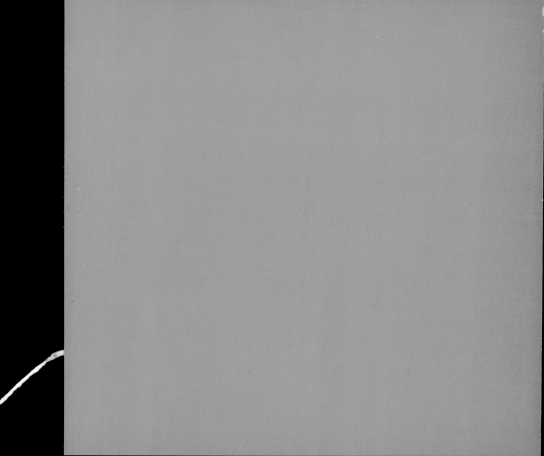

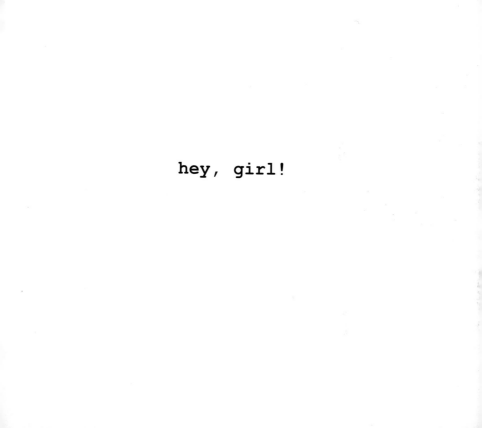

hey, girl!

tim and phyllis

MikWright, Ltd.

**Andrews McMeel
Publishing**

Kansas City

we dedicate this, our first book, to our parents.
without them, we would have been left at the hospital.

ISBN: 0-7407-0493-1

www.mikwright.com

03 RDS 10 9 8

Library of Congress Catalog Card Number: 99-66185

acknowledgments

hey, girl! is a compilation of tim and phyllis's loaded greeting card line, which evolved from family photographs and contributions from their slightly skewed friends. *hey girl!* says very little about the human condition except that we're human ... goofy one minute and ridiculous the next.

the following list acknowledges those who believed in us from the get-go.

to tim and ron from paper skyscraper: thank you for having the guts to sell our idea of humor, which has led to our first book.

to steve, peg, and glenn, our first sales reps: thank you, thank you for waltzing into the arena with photographs glued to irregular-sized paper.

to leona, barbara, norman, and weston: thank you for allowing us to bastardize you, our parents, carte blanche. it's too late to change your mind.

to the folks at andrews mcmeel: thank you for inviting us to play your game.

to bob, our first gluer: thanks for being g.o.d. (gluer on demand).

and finally, to each other: whatever!

yet another satisfied customer
from connie's cut and curl;
where they say . . .

"if your hair isn't becoming to you,
you should be coming to us."

for the love of god, kathleen,
he doesn't care about your hair!
and if he does, maybe he should
be going out with your brother.

big.   bigger.   just right.

that leona was a looker
and the crown would have been hers, too;
if she had only said "world peace"
instead of "fashion first."

listen here you flat chested, broad assed,
penciled-in eye browed, tupperware snatchin'
wench! give me back my deviled egg carrier!

finally, mr. right!

(or at least mr. right now)

oh damn! i wish someone would
invent a fingernail you could just
press on. come on lee, hurry up!
we'll be late!

. . . and then that bitch had the nerve to show up with jello instead of her assigned chicken casserole. now, i'm not one to gossip, but can you believe how fat she has gotten; bitch, please!

i've had it with that bastard!
i'm going home to mother!

love your hair. hope you win!

your mother sure knows how to
work a crowd.

ernest was mesmerized by the size
of clara's zinnias.

yes . . . grandma balked at first, but we
haven't seen a crow since.

i was truly moved by your mother's rendition of "feelings."

do i look like i give a rat's ass?

quit sulking sarah!
at least you didn't find him
with a good looking man.

stylish yet practical,
phyllis learned at an early age . . .
"you don't have to have a perm to
be beautiful."

selling cosmetics dorm to dorm started out as a goof. but, the day they delivered his pink cadillac, david knew he had a future in foundations.

STATE UNIVERSITY

Activity and Identification Card

```
┌─────────────────────────────┐
│                             │
│                             │
│                             │
│                             │
│     FOR CASHIER'S STAMP     │
└─────────────────────────────┘
```

This card is not transferable
and is valid for one quarter
only. Quarter:

David Odum

WRITE YOUR SIGNATURE ABOVE

3578

████████ BOX NO.

STUDENT NUMBER: 63625

WTR. 1966

1 2 3 4 5 6 7 8 9 10 11 12 13 14 15 16 17 18 19 20

like you've never had a bad
hair day?

before . . .

. . . and after.

hence the phrase . . . dog paddle.

as i stand here and reflect, i ask myself . . .
was it right to screw clarence?

step right up . . . just 50¢ to see a full moon
in broad daylight!

it was the last time i ever saw wes.
that night i accidentally glued my
eyes shut in crafts class.

it was nearly impossible to tell the girls apart. fortunately, one picked left and the other picked right.

i ran right over the minute i heard
your mother was flat on her back.

exotic cornfed farm princess in
search of lipstick-dirtbike duchess.
no bi's, no butches.

i'm still waiting for that letter you
promised . . . you lying son-of-a-bitch!

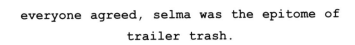

everyone agreed, selma was the epitome of
trailer trash.

it's a miracle she made it.
this is the girl who thought
asphalt was a rectal disorder.

say no more.

esther still stands a little funny as seen here with her flowering bush. just last week she said her hemorrhoids hurt her like a sore-ass duck on a salt pond.

mirror, mirror on the wall . . .
make him rich and make him tall.
cross my fingers and hope for luck . . .
(well, you know the rest)

ladies, i will not stand here and let you talk about poor charlene like that, even though we all know she gets more ass than a toilet seat.

don't be so naive peggy. when marge was
talking about the other white meat, she
wasn't talking about pork.

right now i'm cleaning my oven.

i gotta tell ya, our cruise was great. we danced in the dominican republic, sang in san juan, golfed in guadalupe, and got laid in lauderdale.

about the authors

tim mikkelsen is a transplanted minnesotan now living in charlotte, north carolina. after years in the airline industry, tim now writes and enjoys an occasional vodka tonic. phyllis wright-herman, also a retired airline customer service representative, resides near charlotte with her husband and daughter. phyllis is a coffee critic and the vibrance behind MikWright.

friends for fifteen years, tim and phyllis never lose sight of the role that humor plays in their lives.

triplett-hardman photography   charlotte, nc